Contents

Sketch showing location of walks on back page

Walking times shown inside are approximate and depend on fitness, weight of rucksack, weather, conditions underfoot and height climbed.

Walks 1,7,8 are shown on O.S. Explorer maps No.OL27 North York Moors Eastern Area, walks 2,3,5 on OS No.300 Hawardian Hills & Malton, walks 4,6,9 on OS. No.26 North York Moors Western Area. Every effort has been made to ascertain the accuracy of the walks described. The description of a route or track is not necessarily a right of way.

Some abbreviations have been used in parts of the text to shorten it and make it more concise: -

FB = Footbridge **°M** = Magnetic **RT** = Right **LT** = Left
CP = Car Park **m** = Metres **km** = Kilometres **RD** = Road
PB = Public Bridleway **PF** = Public Footpath

Walkers are strongly advised to wear the appropriate clothing and footwear for these walks.

- Boots/walking shoes.
- Waterproof Jacket.
- Over trousers.
- Small Rucksack containing food, drinks and spare clothing.
- Hat & Gloves.
- Compass & map.

ISBN 978-1-903568-54-5

Walk 1 The Pickering Mill Walk (Pickering)
Walk Time 2hrs 10min   **Distance** 5 miles/8 km
Start GR. 794839 Park in Goslipgate (street)
Terrain A virtually flat walk over fields and finally past some picturesque farms, houses and along past the old mill and beck.

Leaving Goslipgate at the north end, turn left and walk to the end of the lane and follow it round to walk along Manor Drive in the same direction to the far end by the factories (1). Bear left on a track by the factories and continue on the track ahead.

Cross several stiles before coming onto a wide grass track. Continue to the end of the track then bear slightly left, looking for a stile in the hedge on your left.

Head diagonally left (2) over the next field and over another stile. Diagonally crossing that second field to a wooden gate in the hedge line at GR.779824. Cross the dyke and turn left, walking for 600m with the hedge on your left to the access track to Costa Lodge (3).

Cross the access track and walk a further 110m in the same direction to the next field then turn left, to walk on bearing 98°M for 1.3km to join a minor road (4). Turn left on the road, walking parallel with Pickering Beck and following it round past Barker Stakes, Leas Farm and Pickering Mill.

Stay on the road as it passes over Goslip Bridge (5) entering the outskirts of Pickering. Walk along the road by the new houses at the far end, to take you back to your start point in Goslipgate.

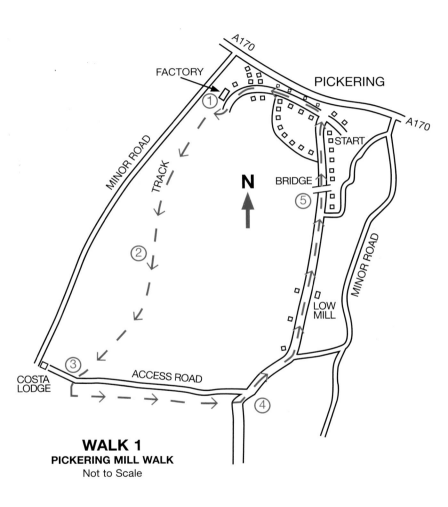

A170

FACTORY

PICKERING

A170

①

START

MINOR ROAD

TRACK

N

BRIDGE

⑤

②

LOW MILL

MINOR ROAD

③

COSTA LODGE

ACCESS ROAD

④

WALK 1
PICKERING MILL WALK
Not to Scale

Walk 2 The Wolds Walk (Malton)
Walk Time 1 hr 50 mins   **Distance 5.1 miles/8.2 km**
Start GR. 865706   Settrington Beacon at Beacon Wold
Terrain A nice walk with very good views but some steep ascents/ descents as you walk from hilltop to valley.

Starting at Settrington Beacon, walk down the wide track marked Centenary Way at the side of the mast and continue to a sign at the bottom, 700m further. Turn right following the sign for Wolds Way then left after 380m to descend to a path junction in the valley **(1)** at GR. 869714.

Arriving at this path junction at the bottom, bear left to ascend out of the valley on a path you can see rising to the top left corner. Walk along the rising path, keeping a line of old trees on your right initially and ascend to the top. Emerging on the top of the hill, go through the corner of the wood then turn immediately left round a ruined farm building **(2)**. Look for the white arrow on a post pointing up and over the hillside at GR. 857712.

Keep the hedge on your left as you go over the hillside. In the next field, cross towards a strip of woodland and cross the minor road there. Descend the access track to Wold House and just before it, turn right to cross a stile just off the track by a large hut, following the yellow arrow.

Descend the steep hillside, bearing right after 150m to a farm gate at the bottom near a large pond. Go through and along the left side of a line of trees ahead, as you ascend the hillside to the top near Wardale Farm. Crossing a stile, you come to the farm access road and turning right, follow the yellow arrow for 580m to a minor road **(3)**.

Turn left descending the minor road for 420m and you come to two large green boxes on your left, which is Settrington Water Pumping Station. Turn left on the track just by there and continue descending to the wood at the bottom on the access track. Go through the thin line of woodland at GR. 848696, to emerge at Low Bellmanear Farm **(4)**.

Turn left just as you arrive at the farm, following the yellow arrows and cross the field on the access track. Entering the next field, walk up the centre of the field, crossing a stile, to ascend steeply up Fizgig hillside clockwise and through a gate halfway up. A further 150m, a yellow arrow points right to a gate. Go through and walk straight ahead.

Keep the hedge line to your right **(5)** as you walk in a straight line for 500m to a track going left to right in front of the woods ahead. Turn left on the track and walk parallel with the woods for 900m back to your start point at Settrington Beacon.

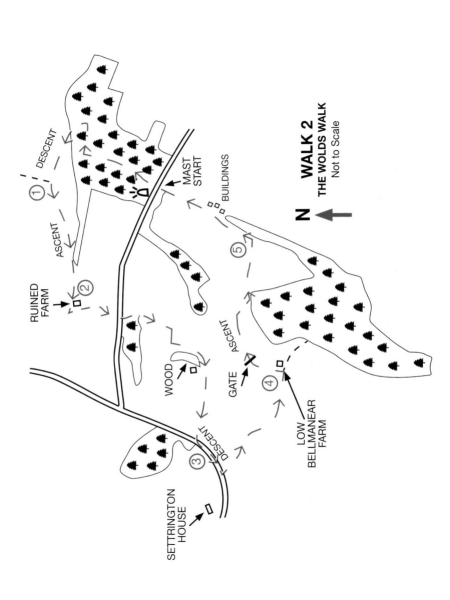

N

WALK 2
THE WOLDS WALK
Not to Scale

DESCENT

ASCENT

①

MAST
START

BUILDINGS

RUINED
FARM

②

⑤

WOOD

ASCENT

GATE

④

DESCENT

③

LOW
BELLMANEAR
FARM

SETTRINGTON
HOUSE

Walk 3 The Malton Round (Malton)
Walk Time 2 hrs 5 mins   **Distance** 5.4 miles/8.7 km
Start GR. 787715 On Railway Street, Malton by the river.
Terrain A pleasant, fairly flat and interesting walk crossing part the old fort area then over fields and through woodland. Some good views on route and old historical buildings in town.

Starting on the bridge over the river in Railway Street, head towards the station and take your first left turn just off the bridge. Keeping the river on your left, continue along the path close by the river to the next bridge by the railway crossing and turn left there over the bridge (1). At the far side, turn right on the bend 120m further, and pass Roman Garth cul de sac.

Walk to the public footpath 100m further and turn left, taking the grass path, which goes diagonally across the field. Walk through into the next field and you emerge on the B1248 Old Malton Road. Turn right and walk to the mini roundabout 450m further (2). Turn left then right soon after onto a public footpath taking you across fields to the far side of Old Malton.

Emerging by Westgate Flats, turn left and walk along Westgate Lane, following it over the A64 road. At the far side, keep on the main access road for 450m then at the far side of a small wood, just before a barrier, take the left turn (3). Walk along that access lane for 750m to the first track on the left and walk up to a house on the left. Just past it, turn right, over a stile by a yellow arrow, and continue along the path for 400m.

Turn left into a field onto a worn path (no sign), then right around the edge of the field. Continue over two fields then bear left in the third by a blue arrow around the field to a gate (4). Go through and bear right towards the wood as you ascend. Cross into the wood and follow it through to the main B1257 road. Turn right there and walk for 100m then cross to take the public footpath through a kissing gate on the far side.

A sign on the public footpath by the road states Malton 1¼ miles. Continue along this for 1.5km to Castle Howard Road (5). Turn left over the A64 then immediately right, crossing a stile to descend a grass path parallel with the A64. At the bottom, the path bears left by some trees and round by a caravan park to an opening onto the B1248 road below.

Turn left on York Road and walk on the grass verge to the BMW garage then continue on the pavement into Malton. Descend the hill on York Road in Malton on the B1248 and turn right 60m before the traffic lights (6), walking down towards the railway station where you started.

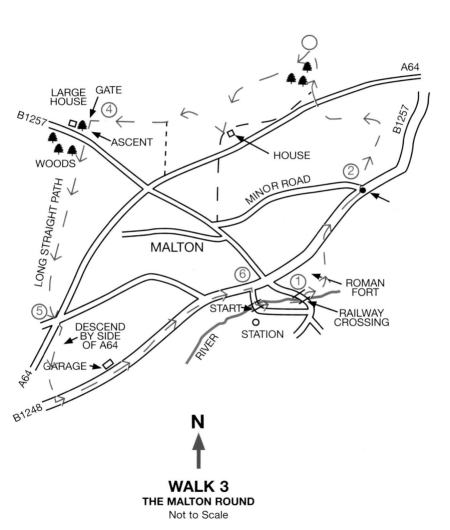

A64

B1257

B1257

LARGE
HOUSE
GATE
④
ASCENT

WOODS

LONG STRAIGHT PATH

HOUSE

MINOR ROAD

②

MALTON

⑤

DESCEND
BY SIDE
OF A64

A64

GARAGE

B1248

⑥

START

STATION

RIVER

①

ROMAN
FORT

RAILWAY
CROSSING

N

WALK 3
THE MALTON ROUND
Not to Scale

Walk 4 Rievaulx Abbey View Walk (Helmsley)
Walk Time 2 hrs 25 mins   **Distance** 5.6 miles/9 km
Start GR. 571844   **Park at the junction near Ashberry Farm**
Terrain A nice walk with good views of the Abbey grounds as you walk over fields and woodland on the circular walk, finishing by passing several large ponds. Some ascents and descents but overall not too steep.

From the junction near Ashberry Farm, walk to the farm and go to the left of it and through a gate with a yellow arrow onto a path, which ascends steeply to the top then descends to a gate (1). There are some good views along this section of Rievaulx Abbey and surrounding area. Go along the field and over a stile next to a farm gate and over several more.

Cross a stile where a sign states 'footpath to Hawnby' then take the lower path towards Hawnby close by the River Rye (2), keeping the wire fence to your right. Follow the path round to a farm gate and onto a metalled track. Turn right on the access track over a short hillside towards Tylas Farm.

On the bend, just before the farm (3), turn left, where there are two farm gates. Take the left gate with the blue arrow on it, and walk away from the farm. Continue on this track, which soon takes you past Tylas Barn and onto the track at the far side. Continue on the track to a public footpath on the left 400m past the barn and walk a further 530m south to the minor road (4).

Turn right at the road and walk along into Old Byland Village. Turn left at the first road on the left, which takes you past the village green in the centre. Walk down the main street with the houses on both sides and round the right hand bend at the bottom. Ignore the first public footpath on the left opposite a minor road and continue to the second one on the left 150m further (5).

Cross into a field, bearing left as you descend a narrow path towards woodland. Continue along descending then ascending the narrow path through the trees for 500m before emerging in a field at GR. 552856. Grange Farm is along to your right, but walk straight across the field, over the farm access track and through a gate.

Walk south for 700m before entering Callister Wood (6), bearing left soon after entering to descend through it to a footbridge at the bottom. Cross the footbridge and over the field onto an access track. Take the path on your left, signposted Cleveland Way and continue along passing several large ponds (7).

Continue until you emerge on the minor road and turn left to walk for 870m back to your original start point near Ashberry Farm.

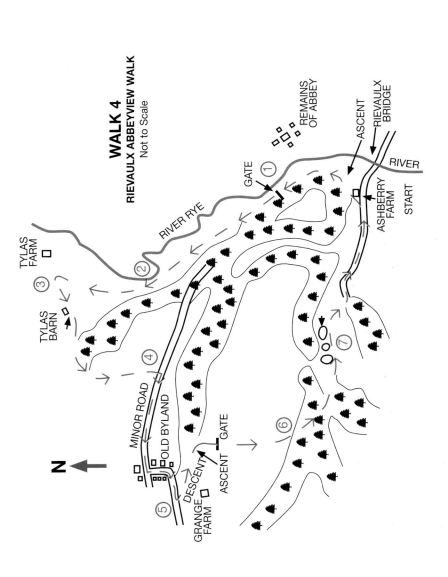

WALK 4
RIEVAULX ABBEYVIEW WALK
Not to Scale

N

REMAINS OF ABBEY

GATE
①

RIVER RYE

RIVER

ASCENT

RIEVAULX BRIDGE

ASHBERRY FARM

START

TYLAS FARM

③

②

TYLAS BARN

④

⑦

MINOR ROAD

OLD BYLAND

⑤

GRANGE FARM

DESCENT

ASCENT

GATE

⑥

Walk 5 The North Grimston Circular (Malton)
Walk Time 2 hrs 35 mins   **Distance 6.2 miles/10 km**
**Start GR. 844677 The Middleton Arms pub in North Grimston on
the sharp bend.**
**Terrain A nice walk following several streams and with a few
gentle ascents/descents. May be muddy at certain times especially
along the track.**

Starting at the Middleton Arms pub in North Grimston, walk to the
telephone box and round the sharp bend with the brook on your left. At
the far end of the bend, a public footpath sign states 'Centenary Way'
by the brook. Walk on the path with the brook on the right and soon
cross stone steps near the old vicarage and continue along the field in
a straight line.

You soon come to Bellmanear Farm, crossing several stiles taking you
around it. Continue in the same direction keeping the wire fence on the
left as you walk to woodland and straight along in a general northerly
direction to Kirk Hill Farm **(1)**. Walk around the farm to the access
road at the far side and turn left on it to descend to a small bridge, cross
then ascend to a junction by Station House 350m further.

Turn right on the lane at the junction and walk for 300m to a road on
the left, signposted Malton. Turn left there and walk for 1km on that
road to pass a quarry, then turn left again just past it at a crossroads **(2)**.
Walk up Langton Lane (track), passing a house and continue on to a
main road, 1.2km further. Walk across the road and through a gate **(3)**
to pass a horse exercising area on your right at GR. 824687.

Continue in the same direction to a road and cross it to walk on a minor
road for 750m to a small bridge by a stream **(4)** by a public bridleway
sign stating 'Centenary Way', GR. 822666. Follow that initially by the
stream then bear left to the far left corner of the field and go through to
the next field keeping the stream on your left. Follow it over a further
three fields as you ascend to a ruined barn.

Go through two small gates just before the barn and bear right, keeping
the tree line just to your right. You come to a minor road by a cattle
grid **(5)**, cross following the Centenary Way signs. Go through another
farm gate and keep just to the right of the small hill on your left as you
descend by the stream to a farm gate under a bridge overhead.

Continue along the field with the stream on your left, back to North
Grimston to emerge on the bend in the village near to where you
started. Turn right on the road back to the Middleton Arms.

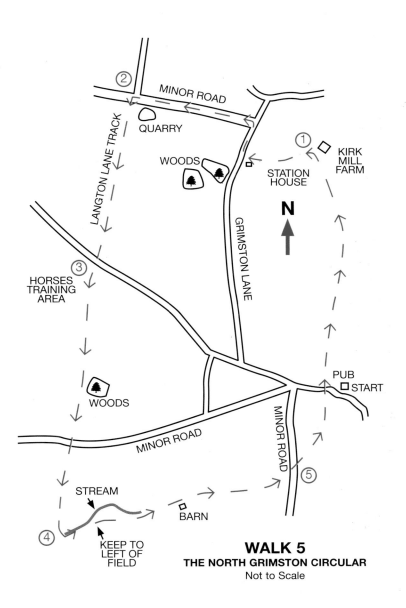

② MINOR ROAD

QUARRY

LANGTON LANE TRACK

WOODS

① KIRK MILL FARM

STATION HOUSE

GRIMSTON LANE

N

③ HORSES TRAINING AREA

WOODS

PUB
□ START

MINOR ROAD

MINOR ROAD

⑤

STREAM

④

BARN

KEEP TO LEFT OF FIELD

WALK 5
THE NORTH GRIMSTON CIRCULAR
Not to Scale

Walk 6 The Ash Dale Circular (Helmsley)
Walk Time 2 hrs 30 mins   **Distance 6.4 miles/10.3 km**
Start GR. 611839 The Parish Church in Helmsley
Terrain A very pleasant walk, ascending gradually through the dale by the beck then a short steep ascent before a gradual descent back through the dale to Helmsley. May be muddy in parts of the dale!

From the church in Helmsley, walk along the B1257 road, passing the houses, to a small footbridge on the right side leading over the beck to a house. Walk a little further past it to a public footpath sign pointing right by a bungalow **(1)**. This takes you on a path by the beck on your right. You cross the beck several times on the way, then at the top of the valley 4.5km from the start, another public footpath sign points right up a steep path.

Ascend, and near the top, a sign points left through the trees on a narrow path. You come to an open field on your right. Continue to the far end of the path where the forest starts on the right side and go through a gate on your right leading into the field **(3)**.

Walk along keeping the fence on your left and at the top of the field go through a farm gate. Turn right along the next field, then left over a stile to emerge on a minor road. Turn right on the road and walk south for 300m to a public footpath on the left. Turn left here **(4)** and continue on this track towards the wood, and to a signpost 500m further down pointing to Helmsley.

Taking the right fork towards Helmsley, descend the path for 3km on a gradual descent on a muddy track through the dale. At the far end of the dale, follow the sign for Helmsley, bearing right through the woodland. Continue through a small gate, taking you along the edge of a field **(5)** then through another gate at the far side and turn right, keeping the fence line to your right.

At the far side of that field, turn left then right at the end as you come to a sports field then left to take you along Warwick Place past houses, to the side of the cemetery. Turn right then first left taking you to the church in Helmsley nearby where you started.

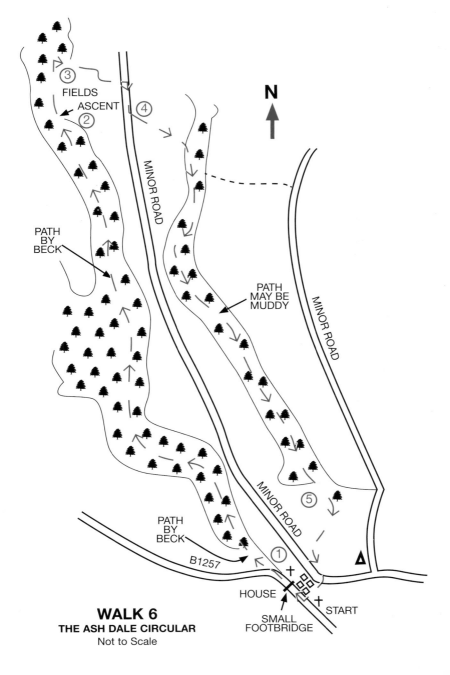

N

FIELDS

ASCENT ②

③

④

MINOR ROAD

PATH
BY
BECK

PATH
MAY BE
MUDDY

MINOR ROAD

MINOR ROAD

⑤

PATH
BY
BECK

B1257

①

△

HOUSE

SMALL
FOOTBRIDGE

START

WALK 6
THE ASH DALE CIRCULAR
Not to Scale

Walk 7 The Thornton-le-Dale Round (Pickering)
Walk Time 3 hrs 15 mins   **Distance** 7.1miles/11.4 km
Start GR. 833833 In Whitbygate, which is the lane opposite the monument in the village centre.
Terrain A nice walk with few ascents, taking you through woodlands and over fields with pleasant scenery.

Walk up the lane (Whitbygate), bearing right then immediately right again where the road forks. You soon descend the lane past the next fork, then when you reach the bend at the bottom by the stream near Thornton Mill and Thornton Dale Bowling Club (**1**), bear left, crossing a small wooden footbridge on your left.

Continue on the path, which runs along nearby the stream in a northeasterly direction over fields. The flat path takes you to Low Farm, where you turn left and walk to the small church (**2**) you should see across to your left. Walk along by the left side of the church then ascend the field steeply in a northerly direction, keeping the hedge on your right.

Ascend through the forest then on reaching the top you emerge on a road through Dalby Forest. Keep in the same direction, passing the tollbooth (**3**) into the forest, (free to walkers!) 600m past the tollbooth, you come to a road/track on your right and some picnic tables in an open area called Haygate.

On the left is a track leading into the forest. Turn left here and follow the track round to a small waymarker sign, then bear left to two small posts with a path between. Walk along the path through the forest to another track crossing yours (**4**). Cross and continue, following the yellow arrow. Walk for 200m to a stile and cross it.

Walk past an electricity pylon there and continue, keeping the hedge line to your right. Go through a small metal gate onto the road (**5**), turning left then right 40m further along to take you along the bridleway by Common Plantation. Walk to the far end and look for a yellow arrow pointing left through a farm gate. Go through then ascend the short hillside diagonally right.

Go through another gate at the top and turn left to walk around the edge of the field to the far left corner. Look for Low Kingthorpe Farm on lower ground and follow the path leading down to it. Go through the small gate and to the left of the farm. Walk through between the farm buildings (**6**) and round to the left of them, passing a round storage silo.

Continue down the valley keeping the thin row of trees to your left. Walk along the lower edge of the fields to a stile 800m further, leading into Howl Dale Wood (**7**). Cross then turn right and continue through the wood on a muddy path for 200m to the far end. Bear left at the end and ascend a short path round to Hagg House (**8**). Walk in front of Hagg House and cross the drive to ascend through woodland.

Cross five fields as your path emerges eventually at the main road (**9**). Turn left then left again to ascend a minor road to the top by a farm. Turn right through two gates and through some woodland before your path emerges back on Whitbygate where you started in Thornton-le-Dale.

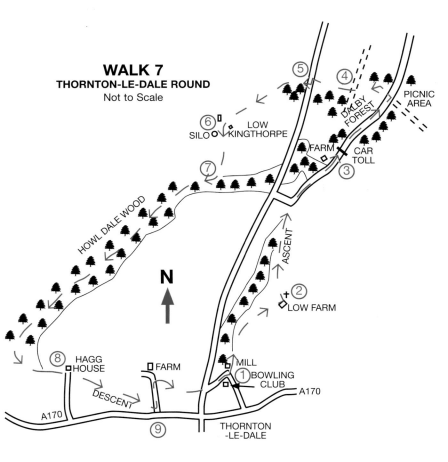

WALK 7
THORNTON-LE-DALE ROUND
Not to Scale

Walk 8 The Blansby Park Circular (Pickering)
Walk Time 2 hrs 40 mins   **Distance 7.5miles/12 km**
**Start GR. 803853 Along Park Road, 1.3km past Pickering
Steam Railway Station in the lay-by beside New Bridge level
crossing.**
**Terrain Quite flat and a very pleasant walk over fields and
through woodland, with some nice views along the route looking
over the fields and valleys.**

Starting at New Bridge level crossing, cross the line and take the
first lane on your right by a house to walk along Blansby Park Lane
for 700m to Park Gate, a house with farm buildings around it. A sign
on the track states 'Private Road' to West Blansby Farm. Continue a
further 30m past it to a public footpath on the left.

Go through the gate to ascend the path through the wood to the top,
then through another gate and turn left (1), keeping the hedge line on
your left. Pass an old farm building then walk round the left side of the
wood 300m ahead, bearing right at the end of the wood. Take the right
track where it divides (2), nearing West Farm.

Continue on the track to pass the farm on your left then cross fields
towards Blansby Park Farm. Go through the gate on the right of the
farm following the small arrow and follow the track round to the far
side and continue in a northerly direction (3). The route takes you past
High Blansby Farm and through the wood ahead (4) as you continue
to the far side. There is a good view down towards a farm and houses
from the far side of the wood.

Descend towards the two houses lower down the track, passing a small
farm. When you come to a farm gate, go through and turn left on the
minor road (5) for 1.1km to a wider road. Turn left again, walking
for 280m to an access road on the right by Lydds Farm (bungalow).
Continue along Keldgate Road (access road) and follow it round for
1km to a sharp right hand bend (6).

Turn left at the bend and head south on Haugh Rigg Road (track) then
directly over a large field in the same direction to an opening into
Haugh Wood. Continue in the same direction through the wood until
you arrive at a short but steep descent on the track in the wood. This
area is the rifle range. Take care and stay on the track observing the
signs, and descend to the range itself at the bottom then continue now
straight ahead through the quarry area (7) to the road.

Turn right at the road to take you back the short distance to the level
crossing where you started.

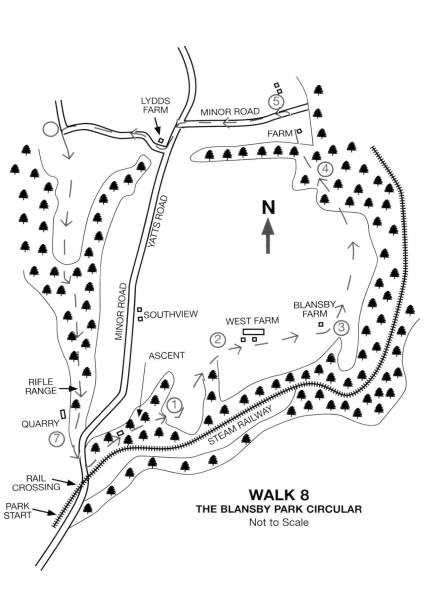

LYDDS FARM

MINOR ROAD

(5)

FARM

YATTS ROAD

N

(4)

MINOR ROAD

SOUTHVIEW

BLANSBY FARM

WEST FARM

(2)

(3)

ASCENT

(1)

RIFLE RANGE

STEAM RAILWAY

QUARRY

(7)

RAIL CROSSING

PARK START

WALK 8
THE BLANSBY PARK CIRCULAR
Not to Scale

Walk 9 Helmsley to Nawton Circular (Helmsley)
Walk Time 3 hrs 20mins   **Distance 9.5 miles/15.3 km**
Start GR. 612838 Centre of Helmsley
Terrain A varied walk with fields, woodland and minor road with good scenery and two places on route for refreshment stops.

Starting in the centre of Helmsley near the monument in the square, cross from the main car park to walk for 380m on the A170 in a westerly direction to the fuel station with a telephone box opposite. Turn up Carlton Road by the telephone box then 90m further, turn right opposite the youth hostel (1) onto a public footpath by a bungalow.

Keep the hedge line on your right. You come to two gates and you go through the left one, following the yellow arrow. Walk across the field and you should see Reagarth Farm ahead on the hillside (2). Look for the gate at the far side of the field and go through to ascend the field by Monk Holme Wood. Walk to the corner of the barns at Reagarth Farm then turn right to take you through the farmyard to the far side, following the yellow arrow.

Walk towards the wood ahead and go through a gate on your right to take you into the wood (3). The path descends the wood and you come to a track. Bear right here and follow it through a farm gate leaving the wood, then cross the field to a gate leading onto the road.

Turn left on the road, walking for 420m to a minor road on your left (4), and ascend it for 1.9km to the village church in Pockley. Turn right here onto a public footpath opposite the church and descend the field, bearing left part way down to a gate in the bottom left corner at GR 642861. Go through, then through the two gates next to it to ascend the short bank through the bushes (5) at GR. 643861.

At the top, walk along keeping the hedge on your right for 200m then turn left on a track leading along the left side of woodland for 280m to a stile. Do not cross the stile but turn right just before it on a narrow path through the trees and descend to the road below (6). Turn right on the minor road and walk for 200m before bearing left on Howldale Lane (track) at a public bridleway sign.

Continue on this track, which may be muddy, for 2km to the main road in Nawton (7). Cross with care and walk down Gale Lane for 1.2km, passing the caravan park then a track on your right. Past that track on a slight bend in the road 250m further is an access road (8). Turn right here and walk for 650m to Shaw Moor Farm on your left.

Turn left along the edge of the field just before the farm then right at the far end of the farm through an opening, then left along the field, keeping the hedge on your left. Cross a stile and bear right following a yellow arrow. Walk in a southerly direction towards Harome village you see 800m ahead. Cross a stile onto a minor road **(9)** at the village then turn right, to walk along the back of the houses.

Following the minor road round, you come to a junction with The Star Inn pub opposite. Cross and walk on the road to the right of the pub for 1.5km to a concealed PB sign on the left. Go through the gate and down the field, keeping the hedge on your left. At the bottom, turn right through the gate **(10)**, just before the railway arch and walk parallel with the old railway line along the field.

You will see Helmsley Castle and village ahead as you walk directly towards it. Continue for 1.2km following the path and arrows to Helmsley. You come to some buildings, turn right, taking you through a small industrial estate back into Helmsley.

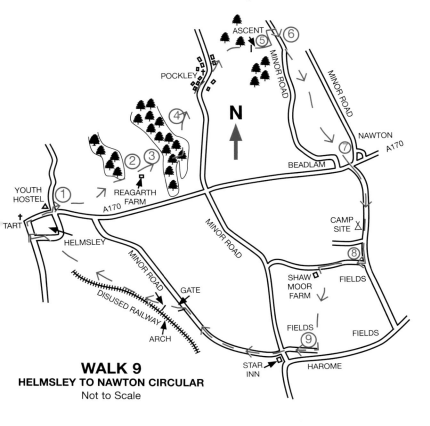

WALK 9
HELMSLEY TO NAWTON CIRCULAR
Not to Scale

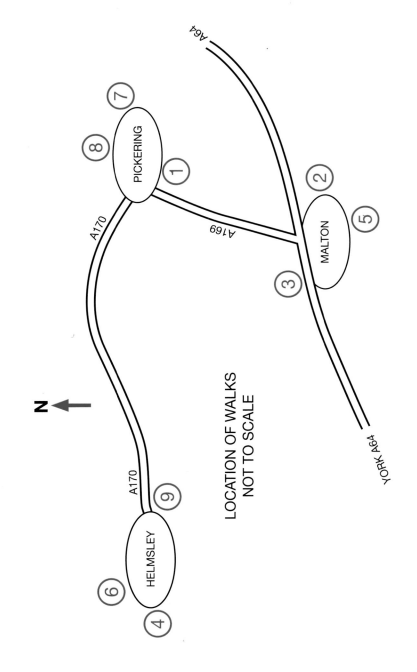

LOCATION OF WALKS
NOT TO SCALE